CONTENTS

INTRODUCTION

If you're reading this, you might be considering a career as a professional barber. As you may already know, a barber is an individual who cuts hair and also either shaves or helps to trim facial hair, styles hair, does facial treatments, and more.

While barbers used to predominantly work in a place where men would just come to get their hair or beards trimmed, times have changed. Now, it is a growing industry for both personal expression and creativity.

If you're considering embarking on the path to becoming a professional barber, you'll have to understand that some pros and cons come with the job. Below, we've detailed some for you to take note of.

PROS OF BEING A BARBER
As with any job, below are some pros to being a professional barber.

Creativity

In the past, most customers would come into the shop and have the barber proceed with a standard haircut that most other men have. Now, that's no longer the case.

While there are certainly some customers that want a simple trim, there are also customers that want a more detailed haircut that even incorporates a design. As a barber, you'll be able to utilize your creativity while testing your skills, so you'll never be bored and will feel challenged continuously.

Every client that comes through that door, will bring excitement as he/she sits down. During the Client Consultation you will figure out if they want a simple trim or if they are looking for the works.

Career Growth

While working as a barber, it's perfectly reasonable to put together a portfolio that details the haircuts or trims that you've done. As you continue to expand your ou can post it online and use it as a way to grow your career. Using Social can boost your clientele much faster than before.

ter you've worked in a shop for a certain period, you can even consider setting up your own shop. While it's definitely hard work, it's also both fulfilling and rewarding.

Having your own shop allows you to do as you please. You make your rules and people that work there with you will have to abide by these rules. If you are a solo barber and work by yourself in your shop, then your whole persona is the atmosphere of the barbershop.

Flexibility

As a barber, you have flexibility in a number of areas. One of the best areas that you have flexibility in is with your working hours. You can choose when you'd like to come to the shop and when it's time to go.

If you have your own barbershop, you're your own boss and can decide when you want your vacation days to be. You also won't need to have a dress code and will be able to set your own prices for the shop.

Make Someone's Day

As a barber, you'll regularly be meeting new people and helping them achieve the haircut or trim of their dreams. There's nothing like the feeling of being able to help someone get the haircut or trim that they've always wanted.

Every time someone sits in your barber chair, it's basically like a blank canvas to work on. You'll be able to unleash your creativity and be in control of the situation while making someone's day.

You never know how the haircut or trim might help someone, it could boost their self-esteem or even help them get that job they've always wanted.

Always be aware that you are changing someone's life everytime you do a haircut. Think about a time when you have had a great haircut and felt like a different person as you walked out of the barbershop and for the days to come.

Great Income

While it could be a little rough in the beginning, as you expand your network and hone your skills, you can rake in a pretty decent income through barbering.

If you decide to set up a shop, it's also important to do some research on the location of where you'd like to set it up as well as the type of haircuts your customers generally go for.

A 2011 study indicated that the top 10 percent of barbers could receive an annual income of $46,000 while a regular barber's annual income sits at around $28,050. Not bad for having the amount of joys and flexibility that comes with this career.

CONS OF BEING A BARBER

While there are certainly a number of pros in being a barber, there are also some cons that you should know of.

Liability

As you're dealing with someone's hair, there are also liability issues that may stem from it. As you work with the customer, issues such as cut, scrapes, patches and even bruises could occur.

When that happens, you'd need to be responsible for the damage you've done to the customer's hair. There's also the issue of a customer not being happy with the haircut you've done for them.

However, if you communicate properly with your customer before the cut (Client Consultation) and be careful when you execute it, these issues shouldn't occur.

Your clients are putting all the responsibility into your hands, and that responsibility should be accepted with love and passion. Grab a hold of the responsibility and do the best you can with every client.

Working during Weekends and Holidays

Even though you do have flexible working hours, chances are, you'd have to work during the weekends and holidays.

It's no secret that a large chunk of a barber's customer base happens during the weekends and holidays as that's when most individuals are free to get their hair cut.

Holidays, everyone wants to look their best for friends and family and for themselves too. If you want to be a successful barber, you will want to take the importance of a great haircut during the holidays.

While you can decide to not work during the weekend, you'll be missing out on a large portion of your revenue – which isn't recommended.

Physical Health

Being a barber is tough work as you're on your feet the whole day. In the long run, this could cause damage to your back as well as your legs.

To alleviate these symptoms, you should invest in a good pair of shoes and stand on a proper floor mat that has a bit of cushioning. Remember to stretch when you're back home and get plenty of rest.

Your diet is key to your success in the barbershop. If you are consuming foods that are causing you to drag or feel fatigue, you may want to consult with a trainer and see what is recommended for your health.

Exercise is also key because it will allow for your muscles to be less tense during the whole day that you are standing.

CHOOSING BARBERING AS A CAREER

The barbering industry is continuing to grow, with more and more barbershops popping up and it is definitely an exciting industry to be involved in!. So why should you consider a career in barbering? Here are 5 reasons.

- Creativity in the Everyday
- Flexibility in Schedule
- Being your boss
- Career Longevity
- Rewarding Workplace
- Barbering is Creative

Are you looking for a job that allows you to work with your hands, creating something unique? Well barbering might just fill that need. Barbering can allow you to craft masterpieces on a one-of-a-kind canvas: hair! Clippers, shears, razors, and more! There's no telling what you will create. What's more is that you can mold and shape a new piece of art on each client, which means you can do what you love all day!

Barbering can be Flexible

Unlike most typical 9-5 jobs, barbering may offer you a certain amount of flexibility in your day-to-day schedule as well as your vacation days and time off. If you decide to pursue a freelance career, open your own shop, or rent a booth, you will probably have the opportunity to set your own schedule. This can make barbering the perfect career for single dads, family men, or men who just like their free time. (Don't forget, ladies can be barbers, too, and they may find the same benefits to a flexible schedule.)

Being you Boss

Bottom line, being a barber is a good life. The job offers flexible hours and rewarding work in a creative industry. Few trades offer as many opportunities to open your own successful business. There are a range of options in how you can be your own boss with a barber career. Some people opt to rent a chair in a salon and build up their client base, chose to work as a mobile barber or open up their own barbershop, where they can really bring in their passions and personality into their barbershop.

Barbering Careers Are for the Future

The Bureau of Labor and Statistics reports that the job outlook for Barbers, Hairstylists, and Cosmetologists is growing at a rate of 10% (which is faster than the average) from the years 2016-26. The opportunities could be plentiful for a well-rounded, hardworking, and passionate barber.

Over the past few years, men's grooming and styling has been more and more refined and popularized. The more dudes jump on this trendy bandwagon, the more in demand barbers will grow as the professionals who can take their look to the next level.

Barbering can be Rewarding

When you cut or style someone's hair or facial hair, you literally change them. Their outward appearance is manipulated, and that's a big deal. With that much power comes great responsibility, and many people thrive knowing that they can make a difference in someone's self-confidence.

You can also make lifelong friends who feel more like family. You will probably see your clients a few times a month, or every few months, and each time they will spend a good chunk of time in your chair. A job doing what you love with people you like? Barbering could be your dream job.

QUALITIES OF A PROFESSIONAL BARBER

Were you always getting into trouble when you were younger trying to cut your own hair or the hair of your brother or sister? Were you the go-to person for doing the hair for friends and family for special occasions?

Barbers are a special breed. They are creative, personable, have an interest in the latest hair styling trends and, most importantly, they have a love, passion and dedication to the haircutting profession.

If you've always had a passion for hair styling, but don't know if becoming a professional barber is your calling, here are some characteristics of quality barbers:

They Possess and Utilize Their Extensive Hair Knowledge

A professional barber should be knowledgeable about cutting hair and anything related to their profession. He or she will use their knowledge to make wise judgements when cutting their customers' hair. They won't automatically comply with the customer's request. If a customer requests a bad haircut, a professional barber will not be afraid to refuse doing the cut. They will instead offer an alternative haircut that will look the best on the individual customer.

In many cases, a professional barber will use their knowledge and professional judgement on every haircut and deliver the customer's desired haircut if it is in the customer's best interest.

They Respect the Profession

A professional barber will love, enjoy and take pride in their work and profession. They will have an unwavering set of ethics they abide by and hold themselves and their work up to high standards.

An example of a barber's dedication and respect for the profession is the refusal to barter their services, doing "favor" haircuts at home rather than at the salon.

They Have Always Have Had a Fascination With Hair

Many professional barbers had a fascination with early on in their childhood. They enjoyed experimenting with doll hair, their own hair and the hair of their siblings. They enjoyed styling the hair of friends and family members for special events such as proms and weddings.

They Are Chatty and Love Being Around People

Barbers and those in the cosmetic and skincare industries are characterized by their friendliness. They enjoy listening to their customers and getting to personally know their customers through conversation. Professional barbers love being around people and serving them through quality haircuts that make them look and feel good.

They Are Entrepreneurial

Professional barbers are hard-working, persevering and dedicated. They are driven to not only succeed, but to also express and exercise their own unique haircutting style. If they can't freely express their unique style, they break out on their own and be their own boss. Many have the work ethic, dedication and drive to become successful business owners.

They Are Creative

Barbering is a perfect fit for those who are looking for a rewarding, satisfying career that centers around being creative. Professional barbers are always current on the latest trends and are eager to try something new. Barbers take pride in the ability to freely exercise their creativity. They are always looking for new possibilities.

They Have a Wide Array of Top-Quality Tools

You won't find any cheap haircutting tools in a quality salon. A professional barber will take their profession and the service to customers seriously. They won't compromise either by using haircutting equipment you can buy at Wal-Mart. Instead, they will spend more on better quality equipment.

Similarly, the barber will have a thorough knowledge of each piece of equipment. You should never hear a barber ask a customer "what number do you want?" for a razor or use plastic attachments that anyone can learn to use.

They are Clean and Committed to Sanitation

As you already know, cutting hair is messy. Touching people's head and scalp can also be unpleasant. The haircutting profession, along with other professions that routinely are touching customers and are in close contact with them, has the risk of easily spreading germs from one customer to another and from customer to barber.

Professional barbers, are therefore clean and strive to constantly have a safe and sanitary salon, even going above and beyond the state sanitation laws and regulations. They will disinfect all their tools after each use, frequently wash their hands, and regularly change their linens.

If you share these eight characteristics, chances are you're on your way to becoming a successful barber.

EFFECTIVE TIPS FOR BECOMING A SUCCESSFUL BARBER

People taking interest in the job of barber might have been wondering about the features and requirements of the barber shop. Have you ever think about a day in the barber shop? Well, if no, you should understand that a barbershop stylist can earn good income through quality services. For this purpose, setting up your goal, framing the complete layout and options of services is the foremost important thing to take care of. Check out these 5 awesome ideas for becoming a successful barber:

1. Set your plans

If you want to become a renounced barber, nothing can be better idea than planning things earlier than your actual actions. Here is the list of utmost requirements in the direction of becoming a barber:

- Choose a good high school for diploma or GED for getting enrolled for the barber course. Also, you will need completing the training and passing the exam with good marks.
- Secondly, take care of being aware about the state license requirements. Also, keeping the information update from the state license authority is good idea.
- Of course, you will have a wide series of options in your career and you can prefer working upon your own ideas. Many barbers are there to offer massage and facial services also apart from their job of hair styling.

2. Ensure entertainment for your clients

During the time you pursue the barber training, you should also learn guts and tricks to keep your customers entertained. Whether you talk interestingly to your clients or you play great music for them, always plan some default ideas for your barber shops that will offer unique identity to your place. Also, be aware about what can be the worst part of your job; for instance, one who is not satisfied with your services will never come back to your shop but if many clients are there to do so, you should research on the negative points of your job.

3. Bring perfection in your work

The only thing to make your services is practice, practice and practice. Initially, you can try your skills on your girlfriend, mother or sister who can become your life time customer if they love your job. In this way, you will be able to check out the level of your skills. Also, follow these ideas for perfection:

- Be in touch of experienced instructors; earlier than getting enrolled in a barber school, take a tour of reputed education hubs in this direction. The instructor should have knowledge of various kinds of men's style.
- Don't forget ever to learn every latest and trendy style for men hair. On the other hand, learning skills to style hair in the most popular designs is an important thing. Good barber training supports you to fulfill the clients' requirement exactly in the way you want.
- Practice a lot even if you become perfect. Continuous practice will make you master of the job.

4. Set up your shop wisely

Setting up the barber shop at right place is also the matter of wisdom. Whether you want to grab good customers or you are willing to get ☐uick response, idea of choosing prime location for the salon is the best. Knowing ideas to keep your clients happy will be an additional advantage.

5. Never lend your tools and books

Whether you are studying or you have completed your barber training, never lend your tool box and books to anyone. Many things are there to be affiliated with this statement. For instance, your friend to whom you lend the book can be late for returning the stuff.

The person that borrows your tools can miss them accidentally and this can be problematic for you.

Hope you got ideas to become good barber through above mentioned points. Well, implementing these 5 basic tips right now on your plan is the idea to start now. This will bring □uick success to you.

We are all the sum of our life experiences, and that also applies to work skills—what we gain along the way makes us better able to fulfill vocational roles. If you mention that your goal is to be a barber, most people just assume that means you learn how to cut hair. Obviously, that is the main part of the job, but there are other things that help barbers attain success in their field.

Communication

Some might imagine that communication in a barbershop would be limited to the basics and bits of idle conversation. However, a barber also must describe in reasonable detail what is involved in doing a particular hairstyle. If the customer does not know what sort of cut they would like, the barber must be able to offer options that both inform and entice them.

Those who have worked in customer service positions know the importance of being pleasant and to the point, while also making sure that customers understand the pertinent details. Those who have worked in publicity or marketing will also have a leg up on the competition in this area.Attention to DetailObviously a barber needs to pay close attention when trimming hair in order to get the cut just right and not injure the customer. However, that attention must extend to all aspects of the shop: regularly sweeping up hair trimmings and cleaning the e□uipment, aiming for a look as clean as your average doctor's office, being well-groomed, etc.

Attention to detail figures into a number of professions. In fact, unless you are a meteorologist, employers expect their workers to get things right most of the time. For barbering, vocational roles where you honed skills such as work ethic, time management, and observational skills are valuable.Physical EnduranceThere are down times where barbers sit around waiting for customers, but if your shop is successful, those are few and far between. You will be on your feet throughout the majority of a shift and frequently be sweeping up the work area.

Previous employment posts with similar work setups include retail, food service and preparation, health care, teaching, assembly line positions, and mail carrier. If you have proven that you can stay on your feet for extended periods in any of those jobs, then barbering should be a snap. If you have a knee or foot condition, or lower back pain, then you will find the extended standing difficult.

SUCCESS SECRETS OF A BARBER

1. Locate the right shop. Successful companies and business owners always have a blueprint. You don't have to reinvent the wheel. There is great benefit in working with mastermind groups. You can glean from the successes and failures of others in your industry. It's important to emulate the patterns and habits of the successful. Identify the top three people in your industry. Don't be afraid to contact them.

2. Tune out the noise. Meditation and visualization are essential steps in feeding your mind. Give yourself 15 minutes each morning and at the end of each day. Take that time to turn down the noise and mentally view yourself accomplishing your goals. You want to fall asleep thinking about your dreams. Your brain works while you sleep. Nwani has practiced these disciplines since 1995. He has witnessed his visualization sessions become reality. He attributes this process to opening the door for him to speak at Bishop Jakes's Man Power Conference some years ago. Make time today to feed your mind, starting with 15 minutes. The results will show up after you become intentional and consistent.

3. Try out new styles. Never be afraid to step out and try something new and different to get the results you want. There are two ways to make money: One is by solving problems and the other is by helping other people make money. Your business model should incorporate both of these methods to maximize your revenue potential. Therefore, Nwani has written books, speaks, trains stylists and aspiring stylists, and consults with others to open their own schools. Think about new ways your business can serve your customers/clients at increased levels.

4. Keep your edges sharp. Daily personal development is vital. You must be prepared to handle the daily trials and tribulations of life. Les Brown, Bishop Jakes, and Michael Hyatt are just a few of the people that Nwani listens to daily. Keep your DVD, CD, and radio station tuned into positive information while you work and play. This will cause your mind to shift. Establish a daily personal development plan, and use it.

5. Don't just sit in the chair. In order to work on your dreams beyond eight hours, you need sustained energy. There is no time limit on the investment of a dream. Some dreams require 10-, 12-, 16-hour days. Therefore, the foods you eat matter. Working out is important so you can have a body that's healthy, nutritionally fit, and equipped to carry out your dreams. You can outwork others when your body is at its optimal functioning capacity. Today, invest in the value of your temple.

6. Go for the BIG chop. Do you know that it takes the same amount of energy to think small as it takes to think big? Be willing to live like others won't temporarily, so you can live like others won't permanently. The greatest investment is in you. Reinvest in yourself and your business to experience exponential growth. Be sure to live below your means now so you can live beyond your dreams later. Get rid of excess and what no longer serves your vision of success.

HOW TO RUN A SUCCESSFUL BARBER SHOP

Barbers do much more than just cut hair. They interact with customers and provide them an opportunity to sit back and relax for a little while. Their easygoing personalities play just as big a role in their success as their hair cutting skills. These barbering tips will help you run a successful barber shop.

Create an Inviting Environment

All clients should receive a greeting as soon as they walk into the shop. If they have to wait, talk to them. Most barbers have a decent sense of humor and are not afraid to crack a joke. Customers will view your shop as a fun place to hang out instead of dreading having to go in for a haircut.

Subscribe to Good Magazines and Invest in a Television Set

Invest in subscriptions to the most popular news and sports magazines. Add a couple newspapers and keep all the subscriptions current. Inspire conversation by tuning the TV to a sporting event or the news.

Ensure That The Barber Shop is Clean

Anyone not helping a customer should be sweeping up hair or cleaning combs, scissors and razors.

Offer Consistent Service

Always open the shop on time. If a last minute customer walks in, make every effort to honor their request for service even if you have to stay open a little while longer. You may receive a nice tip and acquire a loyal customer.

Talk to The Clients

Take an interest in the lives of your customers. Building a relationship will encourage them to return. Be friendly and sympathize with their problems. If they talk about family, you do the same.

Make Your Shop Comfortable

Make sure your shop has plenty of light. Prop the door open if the weather permits. Keep the air conditioner in good working order throughout the summer and use disinfectant so the shop smells clean.

Provide Extras

Performing a shoulder rub and neck shave after the cut is a tradition that most modern barbers fail to provide. Use a straight razor and hot lather on the neck followed with aftershave. Finish up with a brief shoulder rub. In so doing, you will be on the right track to running a successful barber shop.

Provide the Full Barber Shop Treatment

Barber shops were originally thought of as places for men to both clean up and loosen up. That tradition has been around for more than 100 years, so sticking to it is your best chance for success.

A good barbershop experience doesn't end with the haircut. Many men these days are looking for the authentic barbershop treatment. That means that after their haircut, you should treat them to a good neck shave and shoulder massage.

The best way to give a neck shave is with a straight razor. Top this off with quick a shoulder massage, and your clients will leave your shop feeling fully rejuvenated and ready to face anything that comes their way. This is a great way to create customer loyalty, and a great way to encourage your customers to come back often. A haircut is something a man needs once in a while, but a full rejuvenation experience is something that many men crave every day.

Invest in Community

Back in the early days of barber shops, these establishments were gathering places for men; places where guys would stop regularly to chat with the barber, have a smoke, maybe get a shave, and check in with the men in the local community. These days, that type of male community has mostly disappeared. Invest in building this type of community, and new customers will have a reason to come check out your shop.

A great way to do this is to become a community resource person. As a barber, you'll end up cutting the hair of men from all walks of life - business owners, tradesmen, artists, contractors... Become a resource to these people by them to other people they need to meet.

Invest in Atmosphere

Another great way to create customer loyalty and build community is to invest in your shop's atmosphere. Think about what the men in your neighborhood like to watch on TV and what types of magazines they like to read, and make this entertainment readily available. Also think about other things that men like to do when they're hanging out with other guys. How about investing in an espresso machine so you can make cappuccinos for your customers, or putting up posters of classic cars and displaying car catalogues in your waiting area?

Creating an interesting atmosphere is also a great retail opportunity. Display straight razors or other grooming products in your window, and soon you'll have men coming in to ask where they can buy these products. Don't be afraid to get creative with this. You might want even want to sell cigars or coffee beans - if you create the right type of atmosphere, people will want to buy products that help them to create this same type of atmosphere at home.

HOW TO MAKE MONEY RUNNING A BARBERSHOP

Barber comes from the Latin word meaning "beard." Traditionally, barber shops were run by men for the sole purpose of shaving or trimming a man's facial hair. Today, barber shops offer many services in addition to shaving a man's face. Dying, cutting and styling hair is also performed inside a barber shop as a service for both men and women.

1. Set your barber shop up in a location that does not have much competition and that meets your target market. For example, a barber shop set up in an elementary school district would only be ideal if you plan to market your services to young children.

2. Follow all of the requirements set forth within your state permit. This might include keeping the barber shop ventilated so customers do not have to breathe in the fumes from various hair products, or installing disinfectant containers at each station in the barber shop. Experienced customers will not come back to your shop if they notice that you are not following proper state procedure.

3. Keep the barber shop in pristine condition and sterilize all instruments after each use. Customers will not want to continue using your barber shop if it is filthy and putting their health at risk.

4. Hire only licensed barbers that have excellent customer service skills. The talent and friendliness of the barbers you employ will result in repeat customers, and customers that advertise your business by word-of-mouth recommendations.

5. Advertise your barber shop in the town's newspaper, on a local radio station or by handing out fliers at a nearby grocery store. Word-of-mouth advertising is effective, but if you want to reach a larger client base, you are going to need to implement a few advertising campaigns.

6. Build a website for your barber shop and collect basic customer data, including email addresses. Send out a newsletter to your costumers once every few weeks with informative beauty tips and valuable coupons. This will draw customers back to your shop, while giving them the sense that they are truly getting their money's worth.

7. Start a few social networking accounts to keep in contact with your customers. You can use Facebook, Twitter or MySpace to hold contests or post new services that your barber shop is offering. You can even use those accounts to request feedback from the customers that will help you improve the barber shop and meet the demands of your customers so that you can increase your profit margin.

8. Arrange to place an ad in the business directory of your county's next telephone book. This tactic will draw in new customers that you can then turn into repeat customers.

HOW TO PROMOTE YOURSELF AS A BARBER

Successfully marketing a barbershop helps you create a profitable business with repeat customers. The challenge is creating an affordable plan. Most communities feature lots of barbershops and that limits what a shop owner can charge for a haircut or invest in a marketing plan. Low-cost, grassroots campaigns that are highly targeted are best. People are unlikely to drive long distances for a basic shave and a haircut, so marketing plans should emphasize a radius of three-to-five miles. That makes television advertising an expensive waste, forcing most shop owners to look beyond traditional media for an effective plan.

1) START WITH YOUR SPACE

Whether you work at a shop, rent a chair or own your own barbershop, make sure your space sends the right message. This will be a big factor in whether or not a customer will return. Make your space inviting to ensure that your customers are comfortable. It's also important to consider convenience and service. Do you offer great service at a reasonable price? Are your hours comparable to other barbershops in the area? The more boxes you check yes, the more likely your business will promote itself!

2) KNOW YOUR MARKET

You can't grow your business if you don't know enough about the industry. It's important for you to be ahead of the curve and your customers with regard to hot styles and trends in barbering and men's grooming. You'll also want to understand how seasons, holidays, and even overall economics, could impact your business. If you want to advertise and promote your services, you need to understand the really big picture of men's style and fashion. Once you understand the market, you can choose when and how to offer discounts and special promotions.

3) WORD OF MOUTH

Thank your customers for their business and encourage them to tell others they know about you. Word-of-mouth advertising has been around forever because it is one of the best ways to communicate. You never know how many people a single person knows. And when the right person shares their experience about you and your services, there could be huge growth prospects for you.

4) ELECTRONIC WORD OF MOUTH

Word-of-mouth advertising has gone digital! Social media allow you to easily and effectively promote yourself as a barber. Most all your clients are probably on social media, but so are their friends—and theirs! Don't miss this great opportunity. Create business profiles on sites like LinkedIn, Facebook, and Instagram and then start sharing what you do and how well you do it. Get your clients' permission and share before and after shots. Take video and still shots of barbering events and competitions you attend. Post info about new techniques in men's grooming. And share it all on social media. Make sure to pay attention to users who like and share what you're doing. And re-gram, retweet, reuse what they do. A single retweet or re-gram of your photos or stories has the potential to go viral. Even if you aren't insta-famous, you can still get your shop out there, by posting regularly.

5) NETWORKING

Those events and competitions you attend? Don't go without a business card. But even if you can't get in the door to a conference, get online and network. Also reach out to bloggers and business professionals to see if they might want to check out your services and give you a positive review on social media pages. Connect with future clients but also with people doing the same thing you do. LinkedIn is a great place to make professional connections. Find out what they're doing and how they're doing it. Always learn and you'll always grow.

1. Identify key points of emphasis for your marketing plan by creating a SWOT analysis -- strengths, weaknesses, opportunities and threats. List bullet points under each heading to show how you stack up against other barbershops in the area and opportunities to gain an advantage.

2. Obtain a paper map of your area and draw a five-mile radius around your barbershop. This becomes your target area. Find small, local print publications publishing in the area by visiting corner grocery stores, restaurants and gasoline stations to obtain copies.

3. Listen to local radio stations at home or in your car. Try several stations to determine the station that appears to offer the most advertising for stores and shops within your five-mile radius, based on your familiarity with the area. Call the stations to re□uest a rate card or a consultation with a sales representative.

4. Contact the local chamber of commerce for a list of festival and events in your five-mile area, along with contacts for the events. Make phone calls to find out about costs for exhibiting at the events.

5. Establish a marketing budget based on the cost of advertising in small newspapers, local radio and at events in your five-mile area. Look for opportunities costing just a few hundred dollars.

6. Place two-for-one haircut coupons in local print publications. Mark the first haircut up a few dollars over your regular price, with the second haircut free during certain non-busy periods.

7. Create "one dollar haircut" days or something similar at local festivals in your area. Check with event organizers for any special licenses you'll need to give haircuts at the festival.

8. Pay appearance fees to have a local celebrity, such as top radio personality, sign autographs and take pictures at your barbershop on a Saturday morning. Market the appearances with advertising in local print or on radio.

9. Promote a "guest stylist" day. Invite a top barber from a shop from out-of-town to cut hair at your place for a day as he promotes a hot new haircut. Advertise the appearance in advance, and pay the barber travel expenses and a fee for the day.

10. Promote extensively online on top social networking sites and offer free Wi-Fi in your barbershop to show you're really connected to online. Visit major social media sites to purchase low-cost, targeted advertising based on keyword searches.

HOW TO COMMUNICATE WITH CLIENTS IN THE BARBERSHOP

As a professional – it is your responsibility to understand your customer's expectations for their haircut, shave, or beard trim. As you gain experience, you'll improve at figuring out exactly what a client wants, but initially it can be difficult to decode the language your customers use to describe the haircut they want.

Client Consultation

A useful philosophy to keep in mind is that you and your customers are often speaking different languages. The difficulty can easily arise when your client uses subjective language which can be interpreted in a number of different ways. A classic example of this is when a customer asks you for a "regular men's haircut – you know… short" and you give them a cut with a #3 on the sides, and somewhere around an inch and a half on top.

Ask Questions

While your understanding is that a "regular men's haircut" and being "short" both reference something specific – your client might have intended his description to indicate that he wanted to have his hair shorter on the sides and longer on top, and additionally that he expected the length of his hair to be no shorter than half an inch anywhere on his head.

Clarify

While you have certainly performed the cutting of a regular men's haircut (as most men's cuts are conceptualized as being shorter on the sides and longer on top), your understanding of the word "short" may have been entirely different than his. As an uncomfortable result your client may tell you that his hair is now "too short" and he may be unsatisfied with the service you have provided.

The best preventative strategy to avoid this from happening is to continually clarify and make sure that there is a mutual understanding between you and your client. Don't make assumptions about what your client wants, especially if it is your first time cutting their hair.

Be Patient

If you are unsure of what your client is trying to describe, ask them more follow up
uestions until you are certain about their expectations. Remember above all else that this communication with your client is necessary and that it is a part of this occupation. Because of this: it does not work well to become frustrated because it comes across to customers as being unprofessional.

If instead you effectively and regularly clarify with your customers, you will see that great communication is the foundation of great clientele.

BARBERING AND INFECTION CONTROL: WHAT YOU NEED TO KNOW

We all know the scene – well, the many scenes – where yet another paying customer meets his gruesome demise at the hand of Sweeny Todd the Demon Barber of Fleet Street. As queasy as you felt seeing Johnny Depp slay patrons with his straight razor, I think we can all agree it was a welcome relief from the show tunes in this Tim Burton – well, classic.

While this makes for good cinema, the odds of being murdered in the barber chair are miniscule. What is actually a much more real threat to those in the barbershop wouldn't make for a very exciting night at the movies: bacteria, fungi, yeasts, and viruses; micro-organisms in general.

And unfortunately, hair and human skin – especially the sticky, oily skin on the face and scalp – are favored breeding grounds for tens of thousands of species of micro-organisms.

A History of Death by Shaving

While these characters don't usually make the A-list, there are some notable historic cases of individuals who have perished from unsanitary barber procedures. Legend has it that 3,000 years ago King Tut's tomb was sealed with the Curse of the Pharaohs, an incantation that said whoever disturbed the ruler's resting place would face death. Three months after opening the tomb in 1922, George Herbert cut himself while shaving and subsequently died from the resulting sepsis infection.

Henry David Thoreau wrote his famous Walden; or, Life in the Woods after retreating to his cabin near the pond to grieve for his brother, who had just passed away from an infection incurred while shaving. And it's not just razors that can be lethal. In 1921 the death of a former US Congressman in New York was linked to naturally-occurring anthrax bacteria that was found in the brush used to apply his shaving cream at a barber shop. His case was linked to at least 10 other related deaths in the area.

Doing What's Right for You and the Barbering Profession

While public health and sanitation standards have greatly improved today, risks like hepatitis and HIV are real lethal threats in the barbershop. Sterilization, sanitation, and disinfection techniques are the best way to mitigate the risks, and are vital to every successful barber. At best, ignoring proper sterilization and sanitation procedures will get your license or certification revoked. At worst it can be a matter of life and death for you and your clients.

Not only is cleanliness an indispensable part of your own practice, when a barbering establishment makes headlines for the wrong reasons it has a ripple effect across the entire local industry. This holds true for everything from a life-threatening infection to an outbreak of head lice. For the good of your own establishment and those of your barber comrades, you must know and follow proper disinfection techniques. Doing this allows you to concentrate on the reasons you got into this business in the first place: making people look and feel great.

What should be disinfected? Basically anything that comes into direct contact with a client that cannot be easily cleaned, like a clipper guard.

Sterilization, Disinfection, Sanitation: The Methods of Infection Control

Every state regulates barbers and the practice of barbering. Alabama was the last state to implement specific regulations for barbers, signed into law in June of 2015. In the interest of public health, barbering regulations are very detailed when it comes to sanitation and disinfection methods and requirements, so it's important to check the specific laws for where you practice.

Note that in addition to sterilization, many state boards may also refer to "sanitizing," or, "disinfection." While these terms are commonly used interchangeably by the public, technically there are important differences:

- Sterilization – removal or destruction of all living organisms and biological agents from an object
- Disinfection – application of an anti-microbial agent or process to an object, which does not necessarily result in the removal of all living organisms from an object (this is the most accurate term to use in barbering – barbering tools that are reusable are technically disinfected, not sterilized)
- Sanitizing agents – substances that clean (remove oil and dirt) and disinfect
- Sterilization, sanitizing, and disinfection are all part of good hygiene. As opposed to one-time-use items such as razor blades and neck strips, tools like hair shears, hair clippers, and combs are reused time and again. The goal of disinfection is to remove as much bacteria, fungi, viruses, yeasts, and all other micro-organisms as possible from barbering tools each time they are used so they will be clean for the next client.

Commonly Accepted Methods of Disinfection

Disinfection in barbering is accomplished through two basic means:

- Heat – metal tools that have no plastic parts can be heated to a temperature that kills many bacteria and micro-organisms
- Chemicals – these are used to chemically destroy micro-organisms on materials such as plastic that cannot withstand high temperatures
- Some barbershops and salons have approved heat-based means of disinfecting barbering instruments. More common are chemical-based means of disinfection.

When using chemical sprays to sanitize instruments, you must always remember to read what the manufacturer writes about the product on its instruction label (this is important for all products you work with). The typical procedure for sanitizing an object is as follows:

- Remove all physical debris from the object
- Clean the object with soap and water
- Dry the object with a new, clean paper towel
- Immerse the object in an approved disinfectant solution (commonly those approved by the Environmental Protection Agency – EPA)
- Remove the object from the solution with tongs or a gloved hand

As a general rule, chemical sprays should be left on for at least 10 minutes before an object can be considered sanitized and disinfected. This allows enough time for the cleaning agent to chemically break down and destroy the micro-organisms on the barbering instrument.

Once your barbering tools have been disinfected they are ready to either be used on your next client, or to be put into storage. If you're going to put them in storage, your storage container or barber case must also be clean. Cleanliness is only as strong as its weakest link. If your barbering kit where you keep your hair sheers is filled with bacteria, then once you put your hair shears inside for the night they will emerge contaminated the next morning.

The three best ways to avoid storage contamination are as follows:

- Only put disinfected tools and clean objects into your storage case, and have individual storage compartments which can also be cleaned for each tool
- Keep your storage area and individual storage containers closed when you're not using them
- Keep objects in a storage briefcase secured with straps, velcro, ties, or by other means so they aren't bouncing around and coming into contact with each other when you are on the move
- Understanding your state's specific state's regulations regarding sterilization can also help you avoid getting scammed. Some companies market products like barber travel cases that contain, "UV sterilization lights." Based on ☐uestionable science,

many state barbering statutes specifically state these types of devices are inadequate for sanitation and must not be relied upon.

Being Tested on Infection Control During the Practical Examination

Your understanding of infection control and its three primary methods – sanitation, disinfection, and steralization – are under close evaluation during the barbering practical exam you'll take for your state license. This applies to your barbering instruments before, during, and after use, as well as any surfaces on which those instruments are placed. Throughout each procedure of the practical exam, don't forget to begin by practicing good sanitary technique by washing your hands.

During your state's practical exam you will be graded on cleanliness factors such as these:

- Your barbering instruments before use – your examiner will evaluate how clean and effective your storage techniques are for your sanitized tools
- Your workplace – should any barbering instruments touch a work surface, such as a table top, this surface should have been sanitized beforehand
- Your barbering instruments after use – your examiner will evaluate the techniques you use to sanitize your tools and instruments after use

Review your state's practical exam guidelines before you show up on test day. Many state exams require that your clean tools and accessories be in a container marked "clean," and also require that you bring storage containers marked, "dirty," in which you place your soiled materials after performing an examination procedure.

HYGIENE TIPS FOR BARBERSHOPS AND SALONS

Disinfection isn't as sexy of a topic as, say, the latest trends in barbering. It is, however, as crucial a step in managing your reputation as the most Instagram-worthy beard trim or crewcut. Here's how to play it safe with our complete disinfection guide for salons and barbershops.

What Happens When You Don't Properly Disinfect?

In a salon setting, where shaving and cutting implements are in close contact with clients' skin, it is of utmost importance to protect them and your staff to reduce the risk of infection during services. According to the Ministry of Health and Long-Term Care in Ontario, "Exposure to blood or body fluids can lead to infection with blood-borne pathogens including hepatitis B and C, HIV, and other human retroviruses, bacteria and other dangerous pathogens."

What's more concerning, according to Barbicide, an effective and well-known disinfectant in the industry, is that real risks now include "bacteria and viruses that can spread very quickly and be disabling or deadly within hours. We also have the added threat of antibiotic-resistant bacteria (superbugs), which spread very easily, are difficult to treat and can be deadly."

Another factor in the equation is that some clients with medical conditions, such as diabetes, or who are taking medication for asthma or rheumatoid arthritis, are at higher risk for infection because these drugs lower their immune system.

But just because a bug doesn't threaten the life of a client doesn't mean that it can't seriously damage your business. Just think about how quickly news spreads like wildfire on social media.

Three Degrees of Cleanliness

As you might have already noticed if you're a salon owner, Health Canada does not regulate your business or the industry—just the products and equipment entering the country. Disinfectants, which have an amazing track record of effectiveness when used correctly, are classified as drug products that must be approved by Health Canada and have a unique Drug Identification Number (DIN)—something to keep in mind if you are approached with an unknown product or brand.

However, the good news is that you are in complete control of the cleanliness of your tools and your station when using the products and technologies that have a proven degree of efficacy. According to Domenic Sgromo, president of AEMCO Sales, manufacturer's representatives for the professional beauty industry, there are three ways that Barbicide can help salon professionals provide a clean, germ-free environment. "For things like shears, combs and brushes, immerse in the Barbicide solution for 10 minutes to ensure that the bacteria and germs are eradicated," he says. Once the contact time is completed, remove the implements and rinse them with water or keep them in the large Barbicide glass jar on your counter for clients to see. For objects you can't soak, such as a counter or chair, you can use the Barbicide spray and let the product remain, without wiping, for 10 minutes. "Again, notice the 10 minutes of wet contact time, which is vital for proper infection control," reminds Sgromo.

BeautySafe for Best Hygiene Practices

According to Fiona Chambers, executive director for the BeautyCouncil Western Canada, "The lack of regulation poses a risk to consumers if cosmetologists are inadequately trained in the proper use of potentially harmful chemicals and equipment. This is the reason why we have just launched BeautySafe, a program designed for cosmetologists about best practices and legal responsibilities when providing personal services to protect both the beauty professionals and clients."

BeautySafe incorporates standards recognized across Canada encouraging all hairstylists and barbers to be certified and maintain these high standards to reduce the spread of bacterial infections and communicable diseases.The certification must be renewed every three years. "Just as FoodSafe is mandatory in the food industry, BeautySafe should be mandatory in the professional beauty industry—it just makes sense," emphasizes Chambers.

Hopefully, this new program will encourage other provinces to follow suit and auto-regulate the industry, to foster best hygiene practices in barbershops and salons.

3 Steps for Infection Control

Stamp out infection threats with these three simple steps.

Step 1: Clean or Sanitize

The first step in infection control is the removal of visible debris from an object or surface, such as washing with warm, soapy water, or using a chemical cleaner to remove hair product residue.

Step 2: Disinfection

The next step in infection control requires the use of a chemical disinfectant on nonporous implements like plastics and metals and surfaces only. When performed properly, disinfection is effective against bacteria in the salon or barbershop. However, always remember that the disinfecting product must have the proper concentration, mixing proportions and contact time.

Step 3: Sterilization

This final step destroys all microbial life. It's not required in a barbershop, but it's essential in the nail industry. This is always done with an autoclave machine that uses high heat and pressure to kill pathogens.

CHALLENGES FACED BY PROFESSIONAL BARBERS

To put that in context, managing and motivating staff is almost as challenging as getting new clients and retaining existing ones combined i.e. the greatest challenge lies internally within the business more so than in the marketplace.

What is it about these problems that are so challenging?

1. Managing and motivating staff:

Unsurprisingly, staff is the biggest issue. When asked specifically about the challenges, the following were the main pain-points:

1. Keeping them happy within the job and keeping them motivated

2. Getting them comfortable with selling

3. Avoiding confrontation when dealing with issues

4. Consistency of work from day-to-day

5. Dealing with absenteeism as a result of holidays, sickness, pregnancy etc.

2. Getting New Clients:

Interestingly you can see discounting, social media and general awareness were the biggest issues when getting new clients:

• Coming up with marketing ideas outside of discounting
• Advertising and Facebook not working in terms of bringing new clients through the door
• Potential Clients knowing the salon actually exists

Discounting is always a temptation. The reality is though not every client wants the cheapest style or treatment and once you start discounting, it's hard to get back to a more profitable point and get them back to buy at the regular price.

Facebook is also a great tool to drive 'word-of-mouse'. The temptation is to just tell people how great your salon is and run special offers and competitions. But that's where the real value is on Facebook. We have a great resource for salons called 'The Salon Owner's Ultimate Guide to Facebook.' To find out how to get your copy, read last week's blog post.

3. Retaining Clients

Three main issues arose when talking about client retention.

Justifying prices to clients in comparison to cheaper competition

Justifying prices to clients who use home services

Staff not re-booking clients

Again discounting is causing problems. Lowering prices however is not the way to retain clients. Giving them a wow experience that gets them back more often is the fastest way to grow.

Interaction

Although interaction was mentioned in the list of benefits, there are downsides to it as well. For hairdressers in East Brisbane, the interaction with numerous clients every day can become a tiring task and listen to different requests and make sure that each request is fulfilled to their satisfaction is not as easy as it sounds. The reason for this is that not all clients are easy to deal with and that can become a problem when you need to work with focus.

Responsibility

It is part of your job as a barber that the beauty of the client is enhanced through proper hair care and other services. If there are accidents and the appearance of the client is affected then they will blame you for it even when it is not your fault and will not return to your establishment.

Although a barber may choose how long he or she may work, his or her busiest days are going to be the weekends and holidays, which are days usually people really don't want to work. Most people tend to get their haircut around these times so barbers have to work on holidays and weekends which cuts into their free time. If you want a job where you don't have to work holidays or weekends, well, this career can also be for you, just don't expect to make much money if you don't work during peak periods.

Physical health is also very important if you are considering becoming a barber, trust me. Barbers spend almost 100% of their time on their feet, which can be damaging to their back and legs. This can actually affect them in the long run and cause their careers to be shortened, which is obviously devastating if you can no longer do what you love! Even if they feel as if they can't cut another head, they still have to keep the job going. So you will want to make sure you are cut out for a physically straining job such as being a barber. There are also ways to help alleviate any damage that could be caused from the constant standing. Good shoes, and a proper floor mat that acts as a cushion.

Career

Unlike manufacturing jobs, wherein the product your create may become discontinued, people will always need haircuts. Barbershops are located in almost every city, so moving is not a problem. Many barbers are self-employed, so they don't need to worry about losing their jobs.

Work Environment

Barbers usually work inside buildings, avoiding the heat during summers and the cold during winters. Barbershops are typically clean and well ventilated. Barbers don't need to do any heavy lifting. Lung and skin irritations may affect some barbers who work extended periods of time with nail and hair chemicals.

Pay

The main disadvantage with barbering may be its low hourly wage. As of May 2009, the mean hourly wage for barbers nationally was $13.29, which works out to $27,650 a year. This total includes tips and commission. The highest-paid barbers are those who are experienced and have a strong client list. Many barbers do not receive paid vacations or medical benefits.

- Some customers can be demanding and difficult. You will have to learn to deal with them and their criticism of your work without taking it too personally.
- Being self employed means you must take care of paying your taxes and will not be able to collect unemployment if the shop closes down or moves.
- It may take some time to build up a base of clients.
- You will have a lot of competition for other barbers and hair stylists.
- To make a good living, you will have to put in a lot of hours, especially when you are just starting out.

Manufactured by Amazon.ca
Bolton, ON

13121963R00025